lost

&

found

poems by

Tony Dimrajian

this one is for you…

the one who was there all along
the one who never backed down
the one who lost himself
and the one who never did

welcome traveller…

your path has led you to this page
and should you wish to venture ahead…
you shall find an assemblage of words
formed by one often lost in his own head…

who in search of himself uncovered
a myriad of pieces of his whole…
herein dwell the fragments
of that curious lost soul…

in an endless search for meaning
when lost in love, loss and life…
he found in fondness, fate and freedom
a path away from strife…

so lose yourself between these pages
i know it sounds absurd…
but you might just find yourself
hiding in amongst the words…

contents

lost

in

love

i was fascinated by illusions
long before i laid eyes on you

lost in love

waterfalls

    are

       the

          ever-flowing tears

             running

                from the eyes

                   across our

                      lands over a

                         long-lost love

i just have this feeling
that you are about to
make me catch feelings

the way you move
is a form of poetry
i could never form
the words to describe

lost in you

i want to live in your world
where the elements roar
to soar way up into your sky
and sink deep into your shore
i want to dive into your ocean
and dance naked in your rain
to howl at your fullest moon
when wild animals hold reign
i want to challenge your beasts
and feel alive in all my scars
i want to get lost in your forest
to sit and marvel at your stars
and when i draw my last breath
after all is said and done
i want a moment to reminisce
under the setting of your sun

you're still half-dressed
without your clothes
i want you naked
without your walls

everyone you love
was once a
stranger…

… for you can only fall in love
with someone who is
first a stranger

the day we met
you started on a lie
you forced us to forge
our bond on a fragile base   ;
and the more we developed
the clearer that it became   .
we were built to crash   ,
to collapse to the ground   `
to be the bane of a poor   .
architect

we would not build a house
upon a poor foundation
why then do we build soul-mates
upon infatuation?

the untrained painter

you told me it was never to be more than a friendship
i don't know why i thought i could change your mind
i just had this stunning vision of us in the future
i suppose i thought i could paint the picture for you
but now i don't know which was more callow—
that i thought it was the best artwork i could paint
or that i thought i could paint you a masterpiece
when i'd never before even picked up a brush

the only thing i hate more
than seeing you cry
is myself when i can see
it's because of me

i built walls around
us to keep you close
but that only made
you want to escape

you showed me how to live
how to make the most of every day
you showed me that getting out of bed
was always worth the fight
and now that i'm forgetting
i wish you would show me again...

you say
you care
about me
however
you almost
never ask me
how i am
and when
you do
you almost
never stop
to listen

i saved your life
when it needed saving
and then you disappeared
and when the time came
that i needed saving
you came to my aid
so now i wonder
if by saving you
i saved
myself

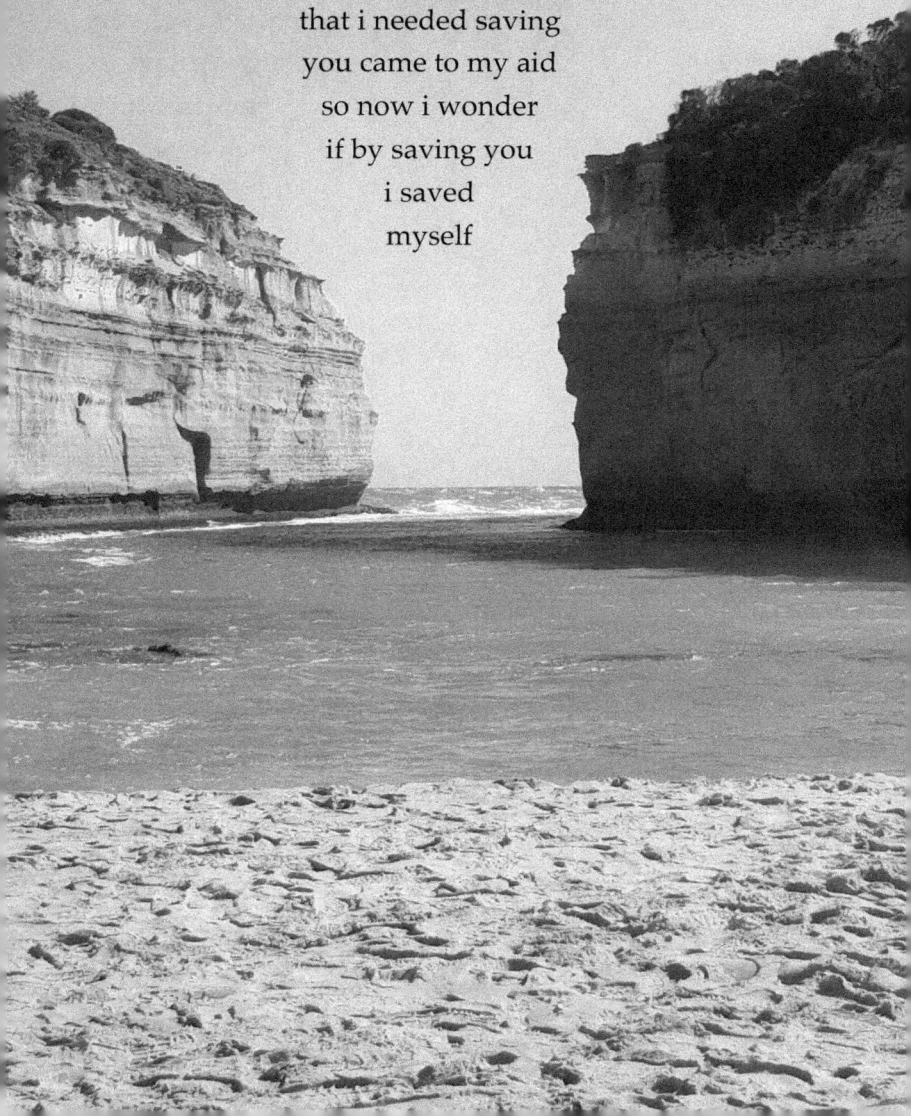

whenever i see you
i always have to
remember to
pinch myself to
see if i'm dreaming
or if i'm stuck
in another one
of my nightmares

today my tears fall
for the man with the broken hands
for he cannot even pinch himself
to see if he is dreaming

random thought #35

what if we are the ones living in the spirit world
and ghosts are glimpses of the world of the living?

it's not always the monster
you hide in bed from
which is most frightening—
sometimes it's the monster
laying right beside you

you went all in
three words in the pot
i'm just thankful now
that i used to play poker
that i knew how
to call your bluff

we tell lies
to protect the ones we love
but that protection
is the lie
we tell ourselves

i think you believed in me…
but when you tried to ignite my spark
you accidentally set yourself on fire
and you burned us to the ground

random thought #18

can you *be in* love with someone
yet not love *being* with them?

YOU CAN'T BREAK MY HEART...

IT'S ALREADY IN PIECES...

even when we're hugging it feels like
we're in a long distance relationship

be *normal*
you say
but
what is *normal?*
is it not just
another word
you use
to make me
do what
you want

if you want to
keep making excuses
then please
just excuse yourself

i crowned you as my princess
i just never crowned myself as a prince
i should've known then it was never meant to be
princesses are not meant to fall in love with their servants

i'm not sorry i caught you staring back
nor am i sorry i held out my hand
i'm not sorry i felt a spark
or sorry i opened up
i just feel sorry for you
that you lost the best thing
that could've happened to you
now that it's too late for you to say sorry

i could never hate you…

…because…

…i could never love you

you are dead to me…

i don't know why you bothered
crawling out of your grave
to try and bury me too

found

in

fondness

apart we are just two sticks
together we can start a fire

the night is over
i said

just five more minutes
begged my friend

but to find you
it took only two

when i first saw you
i remember having this feeling
that i'd been asleep my whole life
and for the first time in my existence
i was waking up to life's epic potential

moment

my time had come
the moment i had so eagerly awaited
the moment i fought so hard to create

and yet here i stood
frozen in fear
mesmerised by her lips

it was now or never
now was too far away
never was far too close

so i created a new moment
somewhere between now and never
where we found our forever

we spoke two different languages
but when our lips touched
we spoke the same

you are so damn uncoordinated
and i am so damn glad
you fell into me

to ignite a fire
you require…
heat
oxygen
fuel
a chemical reaction

the same elements
are required
to ignite love…
searing passion
space to breathe
nourishment
a chemical reaction

it feels like magic—
the way you turn
my t-shirts
into dresses

found in fondness

you are stunning in sunlight

&

drop dead gorgeous in the dark

when i first met you
i thought you were fake
but that is only because
i didn't believe someone
like you could truly be real

you've ruined art galleries for me
because ever since i set eyes on you
every artwork feels underwhelming

i avoid public displays of affection
not because i don't want you
because our spark is so bright
i wouldn't want to blind anyone

they
say
to
get
up
when
you
fall
but
i
don't
see
any
way
for
me
to
get
back
to
my
feet
because
i
can't
stop
falling
for
you

when we first met
you were in pieces
scattered before me

i have savoured
every moment
of helping you
piece yourself
together

you will always be
my favourite puzzle

did i choose you or
did you choose me?
i'll never know…
so i choose to believe
there never was a choice

pour your heart out to me…

…i'll get you a refill

you make me feel so safe
the kind of safe
i haven't felt
since i was the child
who would run
to his parent's bedroom
after a night terror
and sleep nestled
between them

when i cuddle you
i remember—
there is power in gentle

weird

it's when you tackle me on to the bed for
no apparent reason…

or pretend you're about to kiss me but
blow into my mouth instead…

it's when you play connect the dots with
the 233 freckles on my body…

or over-enthusiastically re-enact your
nightmares about the end of the world…

it's when you use a different accent for
every occasion…

or pull that creepy face where you look
like you need dentures…

it's in those moments when you invite me
to be weird with you…

…when we can get lost in our weirdness
together…

…that is when i feel most normal

random thought #239

is it classified as murder
if i make a joke and
you die of laughter?

the only thing as magical
as falling in love with you
was falling in love with you all over again

i have a small confession…
you smiled the first time i snorted
so i may have pretended to snort a lot after that

lost

in

loss

*the problem with having it all is
eventually you have to lose it all*

i thought the problem
was with you
but without you
i have another problem

too young

it tears me to pieces
when i think about your life
you deserved so much more
than what you were given
you deserved to be so much more
than a lesson i had to learn
you deserved love and cuddles
and freedom and fun

my only regret in this life
is that i let all of those days pass
without seeing your face
without hearing your voice
your love was boundless
even though you were bound

now i am most grateful
for that walk we took
when i was too young
to know it could be our last

the only good thing
about you running away
is that now i will never
have to watch you die

i remember how much i loved
spending my days with you
i just hate that i don't
remember much of those days

where now?

where now are the days
filled with nothing but joy...
with awe and adventure
when i could be just a boy...

days of pure fun and laughter
with action and cheap thrills...
where my LEGO monsters fought
and it would always give me chills...

where a bike ride beyond the street
was a journey to world's end...
where now are those days?
shall they ever come again?

my heart beats to the rhythm
of a yearning deep in my core
for a few more of those days
that came so distantly before...

CLUE #1:

While the cat is away
the mice will play

treasure

when i was just a boy
my cousin took my toy

he buried it in my yard
and left me with a card

i came home to find the note
with a clue and a quote…

while the cat is away
the mice will play

yet whilst i did pursue
clue after clue after clue

to uncover my missing treasure
the real gem was the endeavour

random thought #342

i sometimes wonder about what it would be
like to lose your memory…

i think of how horrible it would be to forget
about your loved ones…

but i also wonder just how lucky i would be
to have the chance to fall in love with them
for the first time…

…a second time…

…in this lifetime

i always wanted to grow up
to be exactly like you
i have now come to think
that was never what you wanted
i think you just wanted us
to grow up together

some people are like crackling fires in a snowstorm
you feel warm and toasty when they are close
and like you could freeze to death without them

torn

it is a heart-breaking feeling to be
torn between two loves
torn between two lives
knowing that each could fill your days
but without one
your heart could never be full
perhaps the reason memories fade
is that forgetting gets us through
because it's the only way our bodies know
how to cope with being torn in two

the most terrifying nightmare of all
is the one you find yourself in
after you have woken up

a monster dwells
in each of us

keep it caged
but
keep the key

for a time
may come
when you
need it
unleashed

i'm just myself
in a dreadful disguise

i sometimes feel
at my loneliest
when i am
surrounded
by people

I SCREAM

BECAUSE IT

FEELS LIKE

NOBODY IS

LISTENING

the only thing worse
than feeling like something
is wrong with you
is not knowing what is…

be yourself
they say to me
like it's my solution
but how can it be
when it's my dilemma

depression is not a feeling
depression is not feeling

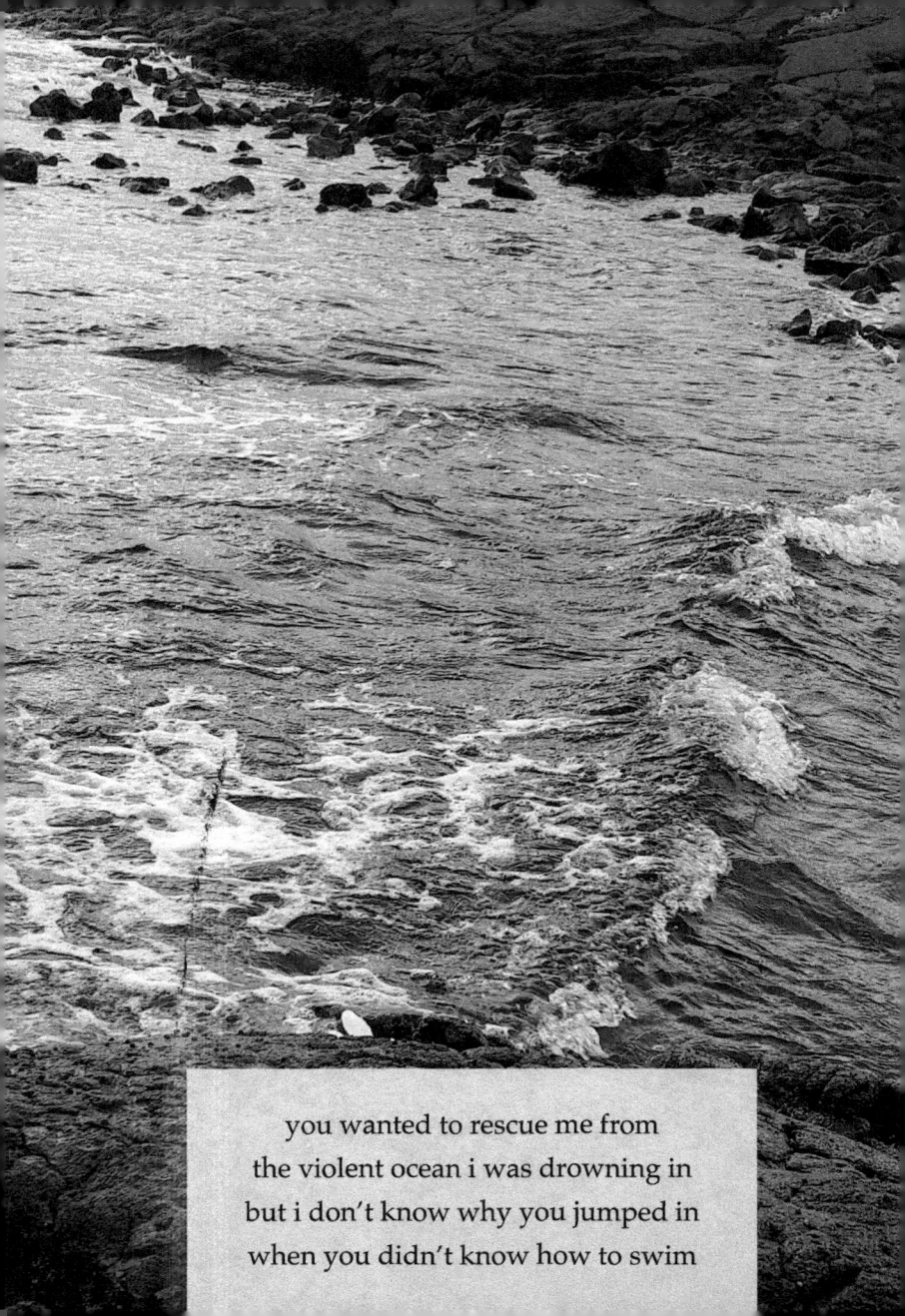

you wanted to rescue me from
the violent ocean i was drowning in
but i don't know why you jumped in
when you didn't know how to swim

random thought #216

it blows my mind to think…

rapists
terrorists
serial killers
were all once babies
they were all born innocent
what vile lives they must have lived
to have learned such a lack of love for life
to have driven them to surrender their humanity
to have had their innocence raped and terrorised and killed

i wonder if the fate of a brighter future lies
in the heart of the storyteller…

if everyone truly knew everyone's origin story
perhaps war would cease to exist…

it might just be that the key to world peace
lies hidden in the telling of our untold stories

every war has a victor   no war has a winner

PEACE

hopeless it seemed…
for i'd failed to recall
whilst you can lessen hope
you can never lose it all

be careful how you use your magnifying glass
do not delve too deeply into your problems
for the more closely you focus on them
the bigger and blurrier they become

i doubt you'll never have doubts

and

i'm certain you'll never be certain

but

i'm positive you can always stay positive

you will have less to lose
if all you do is worry
about losing things

we are not living
if we are not also
in the process
of dying

random thought #46

why should i fear life after death?
i don't recall fearing life before birth

our memories
are the closest thing
we have to time travel
they can transport us
back to relive a time
just never quite
as it was lived
the first time

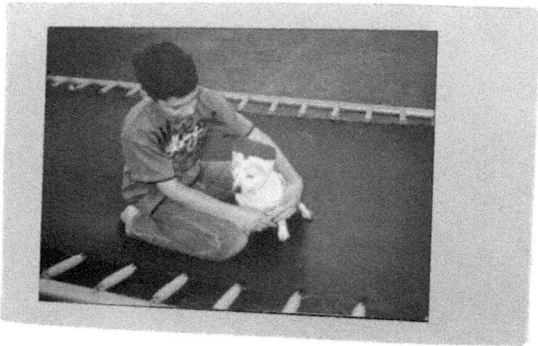

i know it's been a while but...
even if things will never be the same
even if your world has completely changed
even if you no longer have space for me
i still desperately want to see you again
if only for that first warm hug hello

your bags had been packed for many a month
your path was a carpet laid out before you
you were ready for the next phase of your journey
but it was i who was not ready to yet say goodbye
the exit signs were calling you in bursts of green
to this i used my strength to hold up thick black curtains
just one last hug i begged the universe after the last hundred
you were off on an adventure but you were always on my mind

every goodbye you say
to someone you love
is only further preparation
to say goodbye to yourself

we leave a piece of us behind
in every place we visit and
in everyone we touch

i am lost
there is no way
through this torturous labyrinth
have i taken
too many an aimless step
through this internal entanglement
wandering
i am done
for
here i stand
yet
evil has spoken…
turn the tide
and now i shall
die
i will not
rest easy
for i started this saying
i will give it my all
but
life is long until it is no longer
i know that
i am trapped
don't you dare tell me
i will be all right
in this twisted nightmare
i have lost myself
ventured so deep…
oh how i have
steered my fate
what
it is
to have lived searching for peace…
i was never in doubt
i just wish i could say
i had found it
in the face of death…

…read from bottom to top

found

in

fate

*do not let worrying about what could happen
stop you from enjoying what could happen*

i never *meant* to come to this place
yet something within me whispers
that i was always *meant* to find it

dear passenger,

welcome aboard this roller coaster of life
you were not to be the maker of this ride
you are simply on it for one purpose —
to experience the ride
please keep your hands and feet in the vehicle at all times
and do not try to shake it nor direct your path
all you have to do is breathe it in
for however long or short it may last
however dark be the tunnels you pass through
come to enjoy the rush of ascending to greater heights
fear not the sharp turns nor steep descents
for you are safe in this vessel
every hill and dip has a rise and a fall
for without either your ride would not be thrilling
and whilst your cart will come to a halt
once you have followed the path to its completion
let there be a sense of true fulfilment
as you pull into that final station
for you have experienced this unique journey
designed just for you

with love,
the maker

random thought #24

if i tell you to do
what you choose to do
and you do as you so choose
was it ever entirely your choice?

as you follow
the winding path ahead
that runs infinitely through you
past your past and beyond your future
there lies a moment where all things happen...
a time when everything that is to be shall come to pass...
a coordinate on this twisting line of life where all has
ever taken place...

what is this precious moment you ask?

i shall tell you...

...at some point

our emotions fluctuate along a narrow line from
helplessness to happiness
emptiness to euphoria
loneliness to love

sometimes you need
to love feeling sad
embrace it…
revel in it…
it is how we pour
out the negativity
from our bodies
in the least harmful way

i am proud of you
but not of your pride

you claim to be humble
but humility is not
something to be claimed—
it can only be bestowed

core

we do not lose
pieces of ourselves
as we grow...
we rather find them

you see child
it is in growth
that we uncover
who we truly are

for the core parts of us
that will never change
come to make
themselves known

if you worry
about things
that are out
of your control
you will only
make your mind
another one
of those things

everyone is concerned
that i am too fussy…
but i don't understand
why they are so fussed

today i exist
tomorrow i may not
but i've decided today
i'll deal with it tomorrow

random thought #111

perhaps we live in a simulation
made for viewing entertainment

think about it...

what better actors are
there than the ones
who play themselves
without knowing the
cameras are rolling?

i wonder then
if i am a protagonist
or just another one
of the billions
of extras...

art begins to lose its meaning
when its primary goal
becomes perfection

find me someone perfect and i'll tell you why they aren't
find me someone imperfect and i'll tell you why they aren't

you cannot hurry the river
nor can you force it to slow
abandon yourself, come hither
you may only enter it's flow

they say…

     i am afraid of heights

i say…

     no

     you truly fear your body shattering on the ground

they say…

     i am afraid of darkness

i say…

     no

     you truly fear what you will see when all else is unseeable

they say…

     i am afraid of death

i say…

     no

     you truly fear living

     for the fated loss of all that you love about life

conflict is often seen in a negative light but
what good is a story without a good fight?

fighting expectations

every fight can be traced
back to a moment when
someone did not meet the
expectations of another

do not wish ill will on resentful people
instead bear some sympathy for them
for they have been blinded by the shine of others
and now live paralysed in a world of shadow

i'd known you for years
but i did not meet you
until your mouth met
a bottle of alcohol

random thought #90

the placebo effect shows that
our beliefs shape our reality…

or is this just another placebo?

dose
the
highs

&

dose
the
lows

for
everything
kills

when
overdosed

it was not until i first flew
overseas to meet my family
who spoke a foreign language
that i came to understand
how cavemen were able
to communicate love

you had the brain of a four-year-old
but you had the heart of a hero and
even though everyone felt the need
to show you how to do everything
i always knew deep down that you
would show everyone how not to

no *one* is of more
or less value than

any *one* else at all
every *one* is equal

if our
lives
are the sum of our days
then let us make today
a great
addition

make the most of today
someone died yesterday
who will never see it

one
day
i
almost
died

&

now
every
day
is
a
bonus

gratitude
is
the
only
way
we
ever
truly
have
anything

evidence

down my cheeks run the tears of despair
when you whom i love too much to bear
must journey on into the great unknown
it is time for each of us to carry on alone

mortality made me a promise long ago
that there wouldn't always be a tomorrow
now from this day on i will not see your face
not once more shall i feel your loving embrace

yet if this is to be the hour of our separation
let us see what we've built here on our foundation
in this final moment as i hold you tight
be at peace in my arms for this nearing night

once you are gone i will weep to no end
as time passes my heart might seem to mend
though it is not mending i seek when i bawl
for there is much beauty to be seen in a waterfall

i want not to expel the sorrow from my soul
it is more than a reminder that i was once whole
the heartache, the loss, the pain and the tears
are evidence of the love we've shared in our years

anger is just hunger…

for food
for fullness
for fun
for laughter
for happiness
for success
for adventure
for freedom
for friendship
for family
for love

be grateful for what you have
before you want to have it back...

a time will come
when your eyes no longer see me
when your ears fail to hear my call
when your skin can hug mine no longer

and when that time comes
remember—
i am with you
i will *always* be with you
even when you can no longer sense me

the immortals

we do not die when our heart stops beating…

we do not die after all memory of our existence
has been forgotten…

every movement we have made and will ever
make leaves our eternal footprint on this world…

we do not die…

we can never be killed…

lost

in

life

you cannot find yourself
until you find yourself lost

we live in infinite worlds
but with our eyes open
we can see only one

when you close your eyes…
you can do anything you want…
go anywhere you imagine…
with anyone you like…

proof that the universe
isn't just out there
beyond the stars—
it is also within you

if you want to feel massive
look for the tiniest ant

if you want to feel minuscule
look for the tiniest star

i

cannot

say for sure but

when i take a moment

 to stop and to breathe…

  to gaze at burning stars…

 to listen to the burble of the ocean…

  or to sit by the crackling of a fire…

 to be entranced by the sight of a mountain…

  and feel that tug at the strings in my heart…

   …i am taken by a sense of wonder

   and the thought that

   there is so much more

  to this world than

 we could ever

imagine

random thought #127

i have figured out…
nobody has everything figured out…
at least nobody who is willing to tell everybody…

do not trust the wise man
for it is unwise to think he is wise
heed his words yet mistake them not for truth
for true wisdom can only be conceived
in the womb of your own soul

- the wise man

all i know is
i don't know all

one of the
saddest realisations
in life   is the
tragic   discovery
that mum
and dad
don't
have

all the
answers

coddled

the moment I was born
you wrapped me up in a blanket
and since then you have always
sought to protect my innocence

but your coddling has cursed me
your protection has exposed me
for now when i must be independent
i feel inadequate and incapable

the moment I was born
you wrapped me up in a blanket
but you might as well have
thrown me out with the wolves

home is not a place
nor is it a person
home is a feeling
you can find it
in many a moment
only to lose it
not a moment later

you will go far in life
he said to me
as though *life*
can be measured
by some distance

time stops
but time cannot be halted

time flees
but time cannot be caught

time slows
but time cannot be stalled

time sprints
but time cannot be raced

time hurts
but time cannot be harmed

time heals
but time cannot be recovered

time bestows
but time cannot be bestowed

time withers
but time cannot be wasted

i tried learning patience
i just didn't have the patience

i don't have a plan
i don't want a plan
that is my plan

we are caged animals
in man-made enclosures

you say you will do it tomorrow
as you have said for many yesterdays

random thought #4

what if you knew
how many days you had left to live?

would you live them differently
to the days you have left to live?

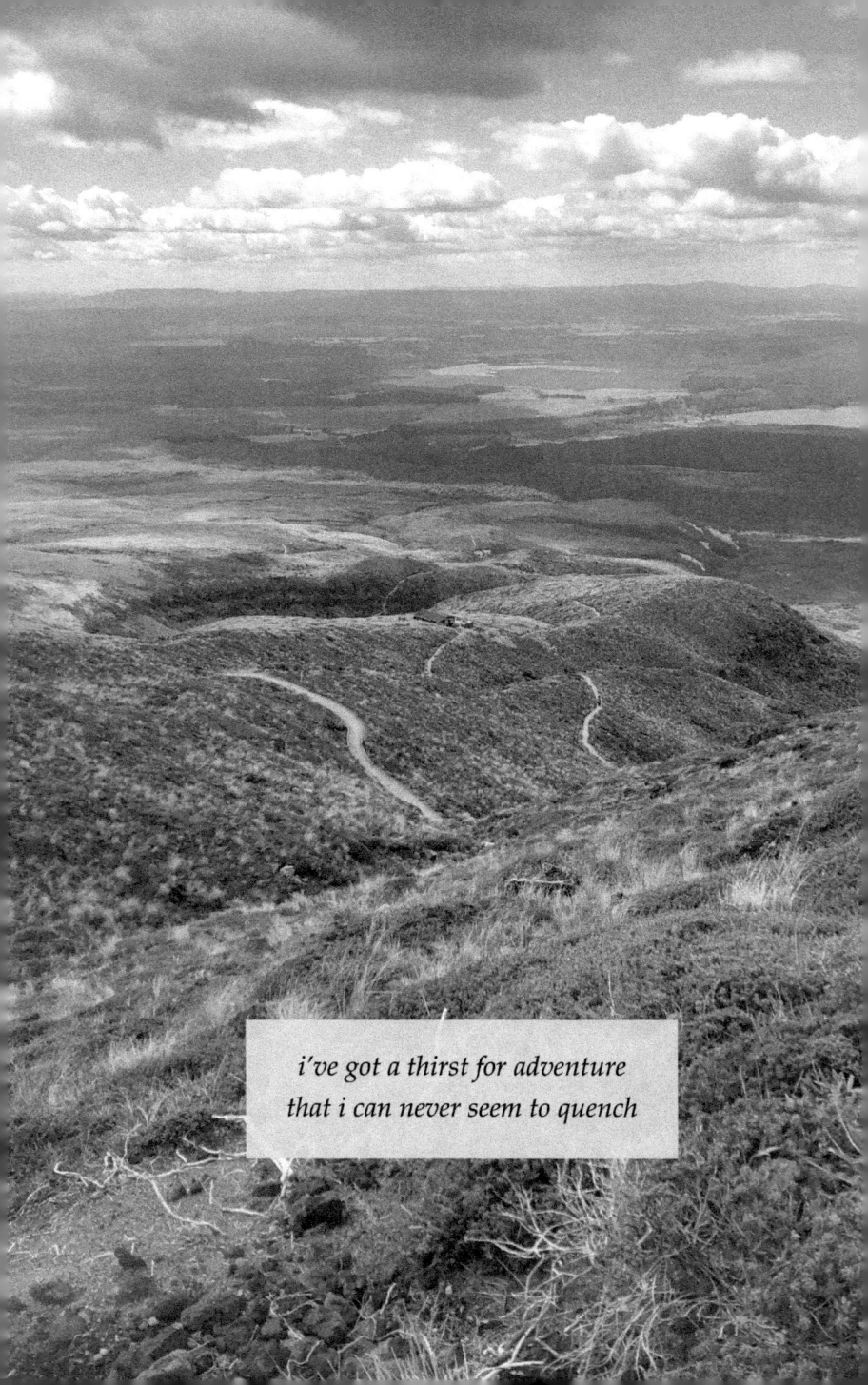

i've got a thirst for adventure
that i can never seem to quench

explorers

sometimes i like to just stop and wonder
what it would be like to be an explorer
to be the first human in history to see a place
to uncover a hidden gem for the first ever time...

yet come to think of it
no human before me has lived a day in my shoes
nor seen the wonders i've seen with my own eyes
not one has sooner ventured into the world i live in

i am the first human in history
to discover each of my days
for the first ever time...

i am an explorer
we are all explorers
all of the time

do not be so focused on your quest
that you miss out on the side quests

the cave

today is lost tomorrow
yesterday is dead
pack your bags and close the door
behold a gift to shed

a new cavern to enter
a new beauty to meet
but pass on through without a light
and nothing shall you see

if everyone became fearless
then it would be impossible
for anyone to become brave

be daring…

…i dare you

some of our
wildest adventures
take place at 4am
in the wild jungle
of our minds

go for a walk through the
forest of your thoughts
to exercise your mind

rain

down
it cries and
pulls you down
below graveyards
to drown in rivers black
to shatter your every day
it screams to stir your soul
something bitter it whispers
a cold voice creeping in
something strange
something eerie
something
sinister

free
it tickles
it sets you free
a pat on the back
it clings to your warmth
it begs you to sail the sky
to dance in waterfalls white
it reminds you of what matters
smiling where your heart lies
somewhere wondrous
somewhere pure
somewhere
euphoric

if death is like sleep
then i'd like to drift off
in the middle of a bedtime story
and dream up an ending
i want the moment before i die
to feel exactly how i feel in that moment
on a quiet night after a long day
when i am so tired
when i am fighting
to stay awake
but i know..

      i can drift off..

           ..at..

              ...any...

                  ...mom—

i awoke in a pool of sweat
from the nightmare i was living…
the nightmare posed as a dream…
that would've drowned me in my sleep

random thought #72

what if we are truly awake
when we are dreaming and
asleep when we are not?

i cannot draw a line to say
what the exact moment was
that i became a grown man
i don't think it was a turn of age
nor a moment of actualisation
perhaps it is just safer
to say i have grown

you are a different person
from the one you were
a decade ago…
a year ago…
a month ago…
a week ago…
an hour ago…
even a few seconds ago…
when you started reading this

the stranger

the boy who adventured did not return
that poor boy was lost the moment he left
days, weeks and months proceeded to burn
yet still that boy had not come home to nest

his mother and father searched far and wide
to find their only son and bring him home
but where that poor boy had run to hide
his parents could not have known

his best friend too set out to find
his long lost brother long outbound
to follow the fading footprints left behind
but that poor boy was nowhere to be found

there was however — a stranger in his bed
who wore his name, his eyes, his skin
the boy who adventured was dead
but could the stranger be him?

found

in

freedom

*i've found
you cannot be lost
unless you've first been found*

we are
only for we believe we are
and so too
shall we be
when we believe we shall be

it's ok not to be who you thought you were
for you are now beautiful in a different way

if this world
    falls short for you
        then live in your own
the one where your eyes are shut
                and your heart is open
the one where you can see a thousand suns
                      setting all at once
the one where you can sit and feel the cosmic river
                          as it tickles your toes
your own wild & wondrous world where nothing makes sense
                  and everything makes perfect sense

take that walk just down the road
to see what lies beyond the hill
to hear nothing but wind
to feel what you must
and then maybe
just maybe
you might just
find some inner peace
if you have yet the courage
to take that walk on your own
that walk just down the tranquil road

it is not selfish
to care for yourself…
only to not care for others

if you can learn
to love yourself
there will always be
someone who does

enjoy your own company
before welcoming company

be with someone
who lets you be...

found in freedom

...without them

YOU
CAN TAKE
A WRONG STEP
BUT IF YOU
TAKE A STEP
YOU CAN'T GO WRONG

dear decision not to leave
i did not make you lightly
the choice to get up and go
was screaming at me quietly
i remember jumping between
being free and being knightly
until i saw i could be both
if i just held on to you tightly

the child competes for the attention of their parents
the adolescent competes for the attention of their crush
the adult competes for the attention of the world
the attentive can see there never was a competition

random thought #12

if life is a game…
what sort of player are you?

the stickler?
the competitive one?
the loose cannon?
the cheater?
the talker?
the completionist?
the sore loser?
the mediator?
the one who sits out?

or perhaps you are the one
who just wants to have some fun?

i thought it was a mistake
and i wanted to take back my decision
the second after i'd made it
but as my feelings transitioned
from overwhelming regret
to overwhelming joy
i came to see—
you were the best mistake i ever made

the only real mistake you can make
is to make the same mistake twice &
even that mistake only happens once

stupidly smart

idiotic ideas…
ridiculous risks…
dumb decisions…
have all led to some of
my most treasured times…
being stupid was probably
the smartest thing i've done

found in freedom

i was so negative…

life felt so lifeless…

no shrink could wake me…

from my slumber of darkness…

then one day it all changed…

one day… i made a friend

we set off on a journey
as domesticated dogs
set free from our cages
and we returned home
as a wolfpack

bromance—
true bromance—
is helping each other forward
and holding on to one another tight
without caring about touching the sweat on each other's backs

envy is the death of love
if you truly love someone
you will feel happy
when they are happy

years of hatred and betrayal
of loathing and bitterness
and to think
it took just a single sentence
to convert all of that *HATE* into *LOVE*

don't count the days or miles
count nothing but the smiles

if you are ever unsure of
who you should keep close
be around the people who
make you smile the most

flirting is not limited
to romantic interests
flirt with the day
banter with the wind
bounce with the waves
play with the energy around you
flirt with life

dear music

you were my first love
the things that you do to me
they are nothing short of wondrous
you have been there for me every time
you never run when i am feeling low
you are always there to calm me
to save me from the darkness
you've taken me to heights
i couldn't have imagined
thanks to you i've been
up to heaven and back
you are always there
without judgement
without prejudice
without deceit
you are raw
i love you
from now
until my
final
beat

the human spirit shines in mysterious ways
if eyes are the gateway to the soul
it is song that pries open the gate
but it is dance that crashes through the gate
like a battering ram

perhaps death is the most daring adventure of all
it could be that just as snakes shed their skin
we must shed our bodies so our spirits
can explore worlds that our bodies
could simply never take us to

do not mistake the end of a chapter
for the end of the story

there is no better time to celebrate
than after you've turned the
final page on a chapter of
your life and before
you begin
the next
one

random thought #151

if every ending
is just a new beginning
will what has begun here
ever truly end?

there is a special feeling on new years eve
that new years day could never live up to
i think there is something about endings
that i love more than new beginnings

when...

when the time for timelessness arrives...
and when you wait less to feel weightless...

when you realise that reality isn't real...
and when the nature of nature nurtures you...

when seeing patterns becomes a pattern...
and when you see how to see without your eyes...

when your emotions motion your notions...
and when you warm up to spreading warmth...

when you live your life to come alive...
and when there are no decisions to make but to love...

...then you will catch a glimpse of freedom

farewell traveller…

i hope you were able to lose yourself
in this passage of pages…
and find something to accompany you
as you venture into the ages…

if there is one final thought we must part on
then this i shall sound…
fear not should you feel lost again
for sooner shall you be found…

acknowledgments

i would like to give a special thank you to…

…Mum, Dad, Gina and Rachel, i am eternally grateful for all you've done for me

…Chief, Shozz, Joey and Matt for your ongoing and wholehearted support

…Melad and Paul for the yute wisdom and encouragement over the years

…the following artists on Unsplash for their incredible photography… Peter Thomas, Dima Pechurin, Dainis Graveris, Courtnie Tosana, Meg Boulden, Hasan Almasi, Eva Blue, Randy Jacob, Timo Stern and Ayesha C

…everyone who has ever supported me… there are certainly pieces of you hiding between these pages… and to all of my readers… i sincerely hope you've enjoyed the journey

about the author

Tony is a poet, writer, teacher and adventurer. He loves travelling, hiking and has a special place in his heart for *The Lord of the Rings;* the tale that opened his eyes to the beauty of storytelling. *lost & found* is his first published work and is an exploration of his most curious thoughts.

about the book

lost & found is a collection of poetry about love, loss, life, death, freedom, transformation and curiosity...

the chapters alternate between losing and finding oneself in the varying facets of life in a bid to shake hands with the never-ending cycle of feeling lost and feeling found...